DK DORLING KINDERSLEY *READERS*

Level 1
Beginning to Read

A Day at Greenhill Farm
Truck Trouble
Tale of a Tadpole
Surprise Puppy!
Duckling Days
A Day at Seagull Beach
Whatever the Weather
Busy Buzzy Bee
Big Machines
Wild Baby Animals
LEGO: Trouble at the Bridge

Level 2
Beginning to Read Alone

Dinosaur Dinners
Fire Fighter!
Bugs! Bugs! Bugs!
Slinky, Scaly Snakes!
Animal Hospital
The Little Ballerina
Munching, Crunching, Sniffing,
 and Snooping
The Secret Life of Trees
Winking, Blinking, Wiggling,
 and Waggling
Astronaut – Living in Space
LEGO: Castle Under Attack!

Level 3
Reading Alone

Spacebusters
Beastly Tales
Shark Attack!
Titanic
Invaders from Outer Space
Movie Magic
Plants Bite Back!
Time Traveler
Bermuda Triangle
Tiger Tales
Aladdin
Heidi
LEGO: Mission to the Arctic

Level 4
Proficient Readers

Days of the Knights
Volcanoes
Secrets of the Mummies
Pirates!
Horse Heroes
Trojan Horse
Micromonsters
Going for Gold!
Extreme Machines
Flying Ace – The Story of
 Amelia Earhart
Robin Hood
Black Beauty
LEGO: Race for Survival

A Note to Parents and Teachers

Eyewitness Readers is a compelling new program for beginning readers, designed in conjunction with leading literacy experts, including Dr. Linda Gambrell, President of the National Reading Conference and past board member of the International Reading Association.

Eyewitness has become the most trusted name in illustrated books, and this new series combines the highly visual Eyewitness approach with engaging, easy-to-read stories. Each Eyewitness Reader is guaranteed to capture a child's interest while developing his or her reading skills, general knowledge, and love of reading.

The four levels of Eyewitness Readers are aimed at different reading abilities, enabling you to choose the books that are exactly right for your children:

Level 1, for Preschool to Grade 1
Level 2, for Grades 1 to 3
Level 3, for Grades 2 and 3
Level 4, for Grades 2 to 4

The "normal" age at which a child begins to read can be anywhere from three to eight years old, so these levels are intended only as a general guideline.

No matter which level you select, you can be sure that you are helping your child learn to read, then read to learn!

Dorling  Kindersley

LONDON, NEW YORK, SYDNEY, DELHI, PARIS,
MUNICH and JOHANNESBURG

Publisher Neal Porter
Editor Andrea Curley
Art Director Tina Vaughan

U.S. Editor Regina Kahney
Reading Consultant
Linda Gambrell, Ph.D.

Produced by
Shoreline Publishing Group
Editorial Director James Buckley, Jr.
Art Director Tom Carling,
Carling Design Inc.

Produced in partnership and licensed by
Major League Baseball Properties, Inc.
Executive Vice President
Timothy J. Brosnan
Director of Publishing and MLB Photos
Don Hintze

2 4 6 8 10 9 7 5 3 1

ISBN: 0-7894-7347-X (PLC)
ISBN 0-7894-7346-1 (PB)

A catalog record is available
from the Library of Congress.

Color reproduction by Colourscan, Singapore.
Printed and bound by L. Rex, China.

Photography credits:
t=top, b=below, l=left, r=right, c=center,
All photos courtesy Major League Baseball Photos except:
AP/Wide World: 4tl, 21br, 45tr, Baseball Hall of Fame and
Library: 6, 7bl, 8b, 9b, 9t, 11br; Michael Burr: 5b, 19b, George
Curley: 5t, 24l; Bill Purdom/Bill Goff, Inc: 10-11;
David Spindel: 7t, 42t; University of Texas: 16t.

see our complete catalog at
www.dk.com

Contents

Throwin' smoke   4

A parade of kings   6

The Rocket   16

The Big Unit   24

Martinez Magic   32

The Ryan Express   40

Who's next?   46

Glossary   48

DORLING KINDERSLEY **READERS**

PROFICIENT
4
READERS

MAJOR LEAGUE BASEBALL™

STRIKEOUT KINGS

Written by James Buckley, Jr.

A Dorling Kindersley Book

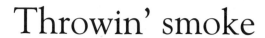

Throwin' smoke

The pitcher stands on the mound, staring in at the batter. The batter waves his bat with menace.

But the pitcher, his face hidden behind his glove, just smiles.

Big whiff
The great Babe Ruth shows what a "swing and a miss" looks like. Ruth struck out more than 1,300 times.

Pedro Martinez of the Boston Red Sox is one of several outstanding strikeout pitchers now playing in the Major Leagues.

The man standing at the plate may have power in his bat, but the pitcher has lightning in his arm.

The pitcher goes into his windup, strides toward the plate, and *zing*, before the batter can move his bat, the ball is in the catcher's mitt. Strike three...another strikeout!

A strikeout happens when a batter receives three strikes, either by swinging and missing or by having the umpire "call" a strike.

Some pitchers turned strikeouts into both an art form and a powerful weapon. These pitchers throw at speeds nearing 100 miles per hour with pinpoint accuracy.

This book tells the story of Major League Baseball's greatest strikeout kings. You'll read about 100 years of hard-throwing hurlers who have made even the best batters shake in their spikes.

Strike zone
A pitch that passes over the plate within the green shaded area is called a strike.

The grip
This is how most pitchers hold the ball when throwing a fastball, which is a key weapon for strikeout pitchers.

A parade of kings

In baseball's early days, pitchers didn't have much of an advantage. Batters could call for whether they wanted a pitch to be high or low, and it took up to five strikes to earn a strikeout.

But as the rules changed, pitchers began to dominate. Tim Keefe was a star for the New York Giants in the 1880s. He won more than 30 games in six seasons. And more than 100 years after he pitched, he is still among the top 20 in strikeouts with 2,560.

Another 19th century pitcher was so good, he actually changed the rules of the game. Amos Rusie [ROOS-ee] was known as the "Hoosier

Like all baseball players of his era, Tim Keefe didn't use a baseball glove.

Thunderbolt," after the nickname of his home state of Indiana. After he struck out more than 900 batters in three seasons, the pitching mound was moved farther away from home plate! It had been 55 feet. In 1893, it was moved to its present distance of 60 feet, 6 inches.

Denton True "Cy" Young earned his nickname because he threw like a cyclone! In an incredible career from 1890-1911, he earned 511 victories, still the most ever for a pitcher.

Top pitchers
Baseball's best pitchers receive the Cy Young Award. From 1956-1966, only one pitcher was given the award each year. Beginning in 1967, a pitcher from each league was honored.

"Matty" card
Pitcher Christy Mathewson as he appeared on an early color baseball card.

What a Rube
Rube Waddell pitched for five teams from 1897-1910.

In 1900, a handsome young pitcher named Christy Mathewson joined the New York Giants from Bucknell College. Over the next 17 seasons, "Matty" created one of the greatest pitching careers ever. The master of the screwball, he could be almost unhittable at times. In the 1905 World Series, he threw three shutout victories in six days, striking out 18 batters and walking only one.

More than most pitchers, Matty succeeded by combining intelligence with a great arm.

Another pitcher of the era relied only on his arm...because his mind was often somewhere else.

Rube Waddell had a rocket for an arm. His record of 349 strikeouts in 1904 stood for almost 70 years. But Rube sometimes missed games to chase fire engines or go fishing.

Another amazing pitcher began his career near the end of Waddell's.

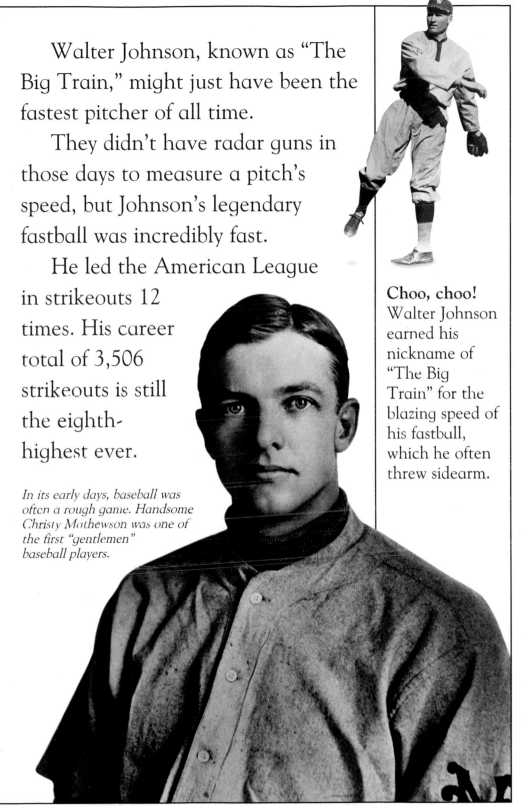

Walter Johnson, known as "The Big Train," might just have been the fastest pitcher of all time.

They didn't have radar guns in those days to measure a pitch's speed, but Johnson's legendary fastball was incredibly fast.

He led the American League in strikeouts 12 times. His career total of 3,506 strikeouts is still the eighth-highest ever.

In its early days, baseball was often a rough game. Handsome Christy Mathewson was one of the first "gentlemen" baseball players.

Choo, choo! Walter Johnson earned his nickname of "The Big Train" for the blazing speed of his fastball, which he often threw sidearm.

You're out!
Some umpires have very dramatic and athletic "strike three" calls.

ERA
This baseball statistic is for earned run average, the number of earned runs that a pitcher usually gives up in nine innings. The lower the number, the better.

Why "K"?
When keeping score of a game, fans and reporters use the symbol "K" for a strikeout. Why not "S"? Because that stands for "sacrifice."

Even as batters in baseball got better, pitchers just kept finding more ways to strike them out.

In 1936, an Iowa farm boy named Bob Feller started one of the greatest strikeout careers ever. At the age of 17, in his first exhibition against pro batters, he struck out eight in three innings!

Feller threw three no-hitters and had a record 12 one-hitters. In 1946, his 348 strikeouts were one short of Rube Waddell's record.

Series whiff
This painting shows Sandy Koufax recording his World Series record 15th strikeout in Game 1 of the 1963 Series.

The kid
Bob Feller, also known as "Rapid Robert," played for the Cleveland Indians from 1936 to 1956 and finished with more than 3,800 strikeouts.

Another Strikeout King was Sandy Koufax. In his short career, he did things with his left arm that are still marveled about today.

During his final five seasons, 1962 to 1966, Koufax won five ERA titles, threw four no-hitters, and earned three Cy Young Awards. In 1965, he set an all-time record with 382 strikeouts. Only one other pitcher, Nolan Ryan, has since topped that mark.

11

NEW YORK — PITCHER

SAM McDOWELL — YANKEES

"Sudden Sam" Sam McDowell earned his nickname because his pitches were "suddenly" past the hitters. He twice had more than 300 strikeouts in a season, and averaged more than 10 strikeouts per game, the most of any pitcher in the 1960s.

Arm troubles forced Koufax out of baseball at the age of 30. Fans who saw him still call him the best lefthanded pitcher ever. While Koufax stunned players with his daring and speed, Bob Gibson struck out hitters with sheer power. The St. Louis Cardinals' righthander was one of the toughest competitors in baseball history. He didn't just want to get hitters out, he

wanted to dominate them. Gibson threw so hard that he often wound up sprawled on the ground beside the first base side of the mound.

Gibson was at his best in the World Series. Over the course of three World Series (1964, 1967, and 1968), he won seven games, had an ERA of 1.89, and struck out 92 batters in 81 innings. The Cardinals won the Series in 1964 and 1967, but lost in 1968.

The mound
After 1968, the pitching mound (overhead view below) was raised from eight to 10 inches off the ground. This helped pitchers.

Power pitcher
On game days, Bob Gibson was like a lion on the prowl. Even his catchers were afraid to speak to him. Here, he is pitching in the 1968 World Series. On this pitch, he struck out his 17th Detroit Tiger of the game, breaking Koufax's World Series record.

"Tom Terrific" helped the Mets win the 1969 World Series. He played for four teams from 1967 to 1986.

Radar gun Devices like these are used to measure the speed of pitches in miles per hour.

In the 1970s, a pair of powerful pitchers were often among the leaders in strikeouts.

Tom Seaver has been called one of the best pitchers since World War II. He not only threw hard (nearly 98 miles per hour), but he had great control.

He led the National League in strikeouts five times, and set a league record with 19 strikeouts in one game. He still holds the all-time record of 10 strikeouts in a row.

Seaver put such effort into his pitching that his right, or back, knee often scraped the ground as he threw. He won three Cy Young Awards and helped the New York Mets win the 1969 World Series.

Steve "Lefty" Carlton is second all-time with 4,191 strikeouts and tied Seaver's mark of 19 in one game. Carlton won four Cy Young Awards.

In the next chapter, read about a trio of power pitchers who are leaving their marks on strikeout history.

Champ!
World Series champions today earn this silver trophy.

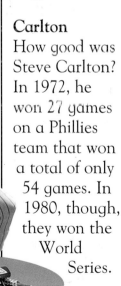

Carlton
How good was Steve Carlton? In 1972, he won 27 games on a Phillies team that won a total of only 54 games. In 1980, though, they won the World Series.

The Rocket

Zzzooom! Whack!

That was the sound of Roger "The Rocket" Clemens firing another fastball past a batter and into the catcher's mitt.

The Rocket's supersonic right arm has made him one of the greatest pitchers in baseball history.

He was drafted by the Boston Red Sox out of the University of Texas.

In 1986, only his third season in the big leagues, he had one of the greatest pitching seasons ever. Clemens led the American League in wins with 24, ERA at 2.48, and was second in strikeouts with 238. He set a Major League record by striking out 20 batters in one game!

And he helped Boston reach the World Series.

But the legend of the Rocket was just beginning.

Longhorns
At the University of Texas, Clemens led the Longhorns to the 1983 College World Series title. He was a two-time All-America selection.

MVP
Clemens is one of only nine pitchers who have won the Cy Young and MVP award in the same season. He did it in 1986.

Two in a row
Other than Clemens, who did it twice, only two other pitchers have won Cy Young Awards in back-to-back seasons. Sandy Koufax did it in 1965-66, and Atlanta's Greg Maddux actually won four in a row, 1992 through 1995.

All-time leader
After only five full seasons, Clemens became Boston's all-time strikeout leader. The Red Sox have been playing since 1903!

After the Rocket's incredible 1986 season, he nearly topped it in 1987. He won another Cy Young Award and had even more strikeouts. At the age of 25, Clemens was the most feared pitcher in baseball.

In 1990, the Rocket had the lowest ERA of his career, 1.93. He added a third Cy Young crown in 1991 with a typically dominating Rocket season in which he led the league in strikeouts and ERA.

Why was the Rocket so good? Well, he threw fast; he could throw the ball nearly 100 miles per hour.

What made Clemens special was his fierce determination to win. He would do whatever it took to win.

Red Sox home
The Red Sox play in Fenway Park, which has a famous 37-foot-tall leftfield wall known as the Green Monster.

A bat?
In 1996, Clemens got his first Major League hit. In the A.L. pitchers don't usually hit.

Eventually, however, he seemed to tire out a bit. By 1996, he had fallen a bit. Was the Rocket flaming out?

Clemens proved that the answer was a very loud "No!"

After the 1996 season, Clemens left the Red Sox, the only team he had ever played for. Boston felt that he was getting older and that they couldn't afford his high salary any more.

For batters
The Triple Crown for hitters means leading a league in home runs, runs batted in, and batting average. Carl Yastrzemski of Boston was the last Triple Crown winner in 1967.

Super All-Star
With Toronto, Clemens earned his seventh and eighth trips to the All-Star Game, held each summer between the American and National Leagues.

Clemens proved them wrong...in a big way. He signed with the Toronto Blue Jays before the 1997 season. Boom! He became the Rocket again.

In his first season with the Blue Jays, he won pitching's Triple Crown, leading the A.L. in wins, ERA, and strikeouts. He won his fourth Cy Young Award. He had the old drive, the old fire, and the same old super-speed.

To prove that 1997 wasn't a fluke, he matched the feat in 1998! It was only the fourth time in history that a pitcher had done that two seasons in a row.

The Rocket's Cy Young Award in 1997 gave him a total of five, the most ever.

With all his success, one thing was still missing. A World Series ring. The Rocket got his chance for one in 1999.

Up north
The Toronto Blue Jays are the only Canadian team to win a World Series, which they did in 1992 and 1993.

Top Tiger
Before Clemens, Detroit's Hal Newhouser was the last man to win pitching's Triple Crown, in 1945.

Champs
The New York Yankees have won 26 World Series titles, more than twice as many as any other team.

Yankee Roger
After he won the 1999 World Series, Clemens said "This must be what it feels like to be a Yankee."

Before the 1999 season, Clemens was traded from Toronto to the New York Yankees.

Fans of the Red Sox were shocked. It was bad enough that Clemens had left Boston. But the Yankees and Red Sox were eternal enemies. It was like watching your favorite little brother move in with another family.

But it just got worse for the Boston faithful...and better for Clemens. The Yankees were a powerful team and he just made them better.

They stormed into the playoffs, and then, to really rub it into the Red Sox, New York beat Boston in the playoffs to earn a trip to the World Series.

On October 27, Roger Clemens finally took the mound at Yankee Stadium with a chance to win the World Series.

The Rocket came through. He shut down the Atlanta Braves, allowing only four hits in seven innings. The Yankees won, and Roger finally got his ring.

How much do strikeouts mean to this King? Look at the names of his kids: Koby, Kory, Kacy, and Kody. The first letter of all of their names is K...the symbol for strikeout.

The ring
This is the New York Yankees' 1999 World Series ring, the prize the Rocket wanted more than any other.

Release point
The spot in space where a pitcher lets the ball go is called the release point. Most pitchers have release points like you see below. Randy's is much farther to the side, and is harder to see.

How tall is tall?
Randy is as tall as 29 baseballs stacked up. At 6 feet, 10 inches, he is the tallest player in Major League history!

The Big Unit

You grab your bat and head to the plate. You step into the batter's box, set your feet, and take a practice swing. Then you look toward the mound to see the pitcher.

What you see instead is a fireballing tower of power.

Randy Johnson, the "Big Unit," combines height, speed, accuracy, and a fierce competitive spirit. These qualities have made him one of the best pitchers in baseball during the past decade.

Johnson stands six feet, 10 inches tall. When he fires his fastball at nearly 100 miles per hour, it leaves his hand almost two feet closer to the plate than most pitchers. That can be an awesome advantage.

Also, his long arms mean his release point is at a more extreme angle to the hitter.

It all adds up to "unhittable."

Trojans
Randy pitched in college for the USC, whose teams are nicknamed the Trojans, after warriors from ancient Troy.

Special card
After Randy's no-hitter in 1990, one company issued this special collectible baseball card.

In high school, Randy was a top pitcher and a basketball player...not surprisingly, given his height.

Randy attended the Univeristy of Southern California, where one of his teammates was future home run champ Mark McGwire of St. Louis.

This is the scary sight that American League hitters faced when Randy was with Seattle, zapping fastball after fastball.

Randy was signed by the Montreal Expos in 1985. He spent four seasons in the minor leagues before joining the Majors in 1988.

In 1989, he was traded to the Seattle Mariners.

As a young pitcher, Johnson was fast, but he was wild. Hitters didn't know if he would smoke a fastball over the plate or over their heads.

In each of his first three full seasons with Seattle, he walked more than 120 batters.

But Randy threw a no-hitter in 1990, and led the American League in strikeouts in 1992.

Suddenly, in 1993, he stopped being wild. Now he was super-fast and super-accurate. When he stared in at the hitter from high atop the mound, he had the confidence to put the ball where he wanted it.

Randy was good before. Now the "Big Unit" was great.

The 'Spos
Johnson's first team, the Montreal Expos, are named for Expo '67, an international fair held in Montreal.

By the sea
The Seattle Mariners logo has the symbol of a compass, which is a device used by mariners, or sailors.

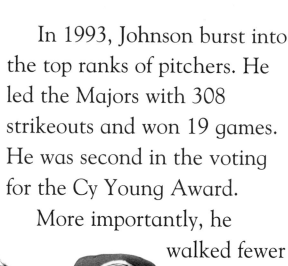

In 1993, Johnson burst into the top ranks of pitchers. He led the Majors with 308 strikeouts and won 19 games. He was second in the voting for the Cy Young Award. More importantly, he walked fewer than 100 batters in a full season for the first time.

Scary good
Lefthanded batters hate to face Randy. In an All-Star game, lefty Larry Walker turned his batting helmet around so he could bat righthanded instead!

New team
Randy joined Arizona in 1999, a team which only joined the Major Leagues in 1998.

The new confidence he had in his pitching made him even better. And he developed a game-day personality that made hitters fear him as he glared down at them.

"Hey, I'm not here to make friends," Randy said. "To get the results I want to get, this is the way I have to be. No one talks to me on game day."

"Randy just stands up there and says 'I'm in charge,'" says Boston slugger Mo Vaughn. "And he is."

The former wild man continued to improve.

In 1995, the Big Unit won the Cy Young Award, while Seattle made the playoffs.

After suffering through a back injury in 1996, Johnson came back strong in 1997 with his first 20-win season. He also struck out 19 batters in one game.

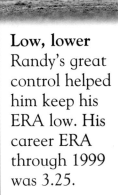

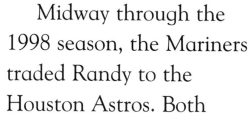

Quick trip
Randy spent only six months with the Astros, but he helped them reach the National League playoffs.

Big strike zone
Because he is now in the National League, Randy has to bat. A.L. teams use a designated hitter.

Midway through the 1998 season, the Mariners traded Randy to the Houston Astros. Both Seattle and Randy had become unhappy with each other, and it was time for a change.

The change did Johnson good. With Houston, he was 10-1 in just half a season; his total of 329 strikeouts led the Majors.

Energized by his time with the Astros, but wanting to be near his offseason home in Arizona, he signed with the Diamondbacks for 1999.

The Big Unit picked up right where he left off. In 1999, he became the third pitcher to win the Cy Young Award in each league, and he set a new career high with 364 strikeouts.

Randy Johnson might be getting older, but he's still getting better.

The Big Unit had more strikeouts than any other pitcher in the 1990s, and one of the lowest ERAs. But what was more important than all the batters he "punched out" was the way he continued to improve every season.

Randy's "heater" and desire to win helped make Arizona one of the N.L.'s top teams.

Snaky symbol
The Arizona Diamondbacks play their home games in Phoenix. The diamondback is a deadly snake that lives in the desert.

Another victim
Cleveland's Manny Ramirez had an incredible 165 RBI in 1999, but against Pedro he is only 3 for 23.

Pedro's home country
The Dominican Republic is a country on an island in the Caribbean Sea.

Martinez Magic

If you're his teammate, you're his friend. Ace Red Sox pitcher Pedro Martinez is a great guy to be around, always laughing and joking and playing tricks.

But if you're an opponent with a bat in your hand...watch out!

"Pedro has no fear out there," says teammate Carl Everett.

The only fear comes from the hitters who must face him.

"He's a nightmare," says Seattle slugger Jay Buhner. "I'm not playing against him anymore."

Buhner has faced Pedro eight times...and struck out all eight times. Ken Griffey, Jr., has never had a hit against Pedro.

How does Pedro do it? He has created a dizzying selection of pitches that make him one of the best in the game.

Pedro Martinez grew up in the Dominican Republic, a nation where baseball is king. He signed a contract with the Los Angeles Dodgers when he was 17 years old.

He was the Minor League Player of the Year in 1991 and became a Dodgers' regular in 1993.

Sign here
Baseball players sign contracts with a team. The teams then send the players to the minors to improve before joining the Major League club.

A young Pedro Martinez fires a fastball for Montreal.

Although he pitched well for the Dodgers, the team felt he was too skinny to become very successful. So they traded him to the Montreal Expos.

With Montreal, Pedro became a star, and he increased his strikeout total every year.

In a 1995 game, he showed signs of his future greatness when he nearly pitched a perfect game. Only a 10th-inning hit spoiled it.

In 1996, Pedro pitched a game against the Dodgers. The opposing pitcher was his brother, Ramon, who had once been his teammate in Los Angeles. It was only the sixth time in history that brothers had pitched against one another. Ramon won, but Pedro would soon overshadow his older brother.

Other brothers
Phil and Joe Niekro are perhaps the most famous pair of pitching brothers. Both specialized in the knuckleball, and Phil is now in the Baseball Hall of Fame.

Perfect game
This rare pitching feat occurs when a pitcher allows no baserunners of any kind through an entire game.

Pedro's finest season yet came in 1997. His 305 strikeouts made him the first pitcher from Latin America to reach that total. He was the first righthanded pitcher with 300 strikeouts and an ERA under 2.00 (his was 1.90) in one season since Walter Johnson in 1912! Surprisingly, he was traded to the Boston Red Sox after the season. But a new league didn't change Pedro's style. He struck out 251 batters in 1998, and helped the Red Sox by winning the first game of the playoffs.

Entering 1999, many people were expecting big things from Pedro. But he didn't let the pressure bother him. In fact, he put on one of the greatest displays of pitching excellence in baseball history.

In 1999, it was Pedro's turn to win pitching's Triple Crown.

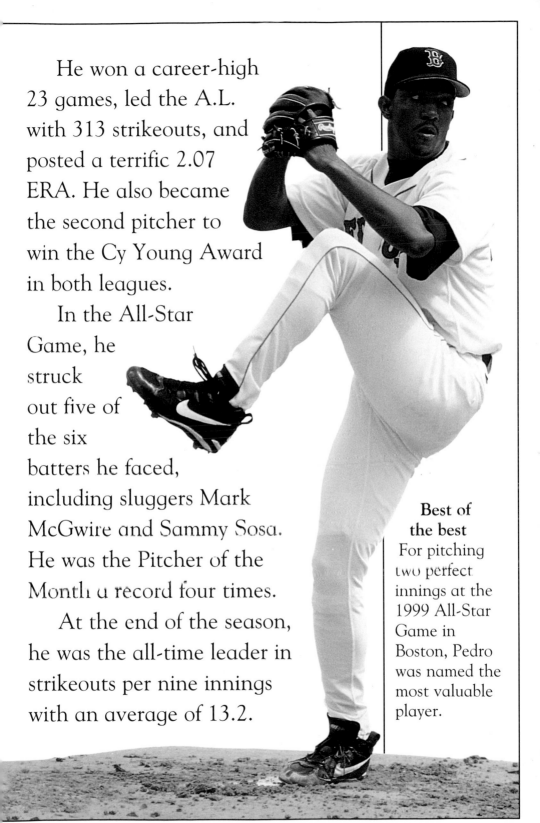

He won a career-high 23 games, led the A.L. with 313 strikeouts, and posted a terrific 2.07 ERA. He also became the second pitcher to win the Cy Young Award in both leagues.

In the All-Star Game, he struck out five of the six batters he faced, including sluggers Mark McGwire and Sammy Sosa. He was the Pitcher of the Month a record four times.

At the end of the season, he was the all-time leader in strikeouts per nine innings with an average of 13.2.

Best of the best
For pitching two perfect innings at the 1999 All-Star Game in Boston, Pedro was named the most valuable player.

Together again
Pedro was reunited on the Red Sox with his brother Ramon. Together, they helped the Red Sox make the playoffs twice.

Bullpen
Relief pitchers get ready to come into the game in an area of the field called the bullpen.

Perhaps most amazing about Pedro's 1999 season was his control. He had nearly 10 strikeouts for every walk he allowed. Strikeout pitchers have been around for many years, but few have had Pedro's ability to pitch accurately.

He saved his best for last. In an important game against the Yankees, Pedro struck out 17. The big win helped the Red Sox earn a wild-card spot in the playoffs.

In the American League Division Series, he came out of the bullpen in the crucial Game 5 to pitch five perfect innings to seal the win.

And in the A.L. Championship Series, in a packed and screaming Fenway Park, he dueled fellow strikeout ace Roger Clemens...and won a big game for the Red Sox.

AMERICAN LEAGUE

	1	2	3	4	5	6	7	8	9	10	R	H	E	P	
SEA	0	0	0		0	0	0	0			0	2	1	35	BAL
BOSTON	1	0	3		1	0	0	0			5	13	0	22	DET

| | | | | | | | | 19 | ANA |
| 41 | CLE |
BAT BALL STRIKE OUT (H)   (E) | 29 | OAK |
| 46 | NY |

At home
This painting shows Pedro about to fire a pitch toward home plate at Fenway Park. The scoreboard behind him is not electronic, but is run by a person sitting inside the wall behind it. Most scoreboards today are operated from a booth inside the stadium press box, rather than by hand.

When the pressure is on, Pedro comes through...and then he and his teammates start smiling again.

It's the batters who won't be wearing any smiles.

Hometown kid does good
After he became a successful pitcher, Pedro helped the folks back home in Manoguayabo, D.R., by building them a new church.

Young star
Ryan helped
the New York
Mets win the
World Series in
1969, a victory
so surprising
the team was
called the
"Miracle Mets."

The Ryan Express

Cy Young. Matty. The Big Train.
Koufax. Seaver. Lefty. The Rocket.
Pedro. The Big Unit.

Baseball history is filled with
strikeout superstars like those
players. But one pitcher
stands head and shoulders
above the rest as the King of
the Strikeout Kings.

Nolan Ryan finished his
amazing career in 1993 after
a record 27 seasons with a
flabbergasting 5,714 total
strikeouts!

A big, humble fellow
from little Alvin, Texas, Ryan had
one of the most powerful fastballs
in baseball history. He also had
the ability to throw it at top speed
over and over again.

Ryan pitched until he was 46
years old, more than a decade past
the age most pitchers retire.

**Other side of
the coin**
Along with
holding the
record for most
strikeouts, Ryan
walked the
most batters
ever, too:
2,795.

Number seven
This ball was used in Nolan Ryan's seventh no-hitter, in 1991 against Toronto when he was 44 years old.

Some good years
Ryan pitched for the Houston Astros from 1980-1988. He had a career low ERA of 1.69 with them in 1981.

Along with his barrels full of strikeouts, Ryan did something that is perhaps even more amazing. He threw seven no-hitters! No other pitcher even has five in his career.

Ryan began his career with the New York Mets. From the start, Ryan had a fiery fastball, but he was wild.

He didn't do that well for the Mets, and in 1972 they traded him to the California Angels.

Ryan quickly proved that the Mets had made a big mistake. From 1972-1974 his strikeout totals were 329, 383 (a new Major League record), and 367. He won at least 19 games in each of those seasons.

The Ryan Express was taking off for the big time!

Throughout the 1970s, he dominated batters, leading the Majors in strikeouts four more times in the decade.

By the end of the 1970s, for some reason, the Angels thought Ryan was getting too old. Shows how much they knew...he pitched for 14 more seasons—and had 2,805 more strikeouts—after they traded him to the Houston Astros in 1979.

A big one
The 5,000th strikeout of Ryan's career came in 1989 against Rickey Henderson.

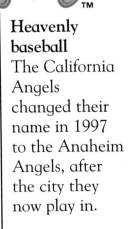

Heavenly baseball
The California Angels changed their name in 1997 to the Anaheim Angels, after the city they now play in.

New team
After he retired from the Majors, Ryan stayed active in baseball, buying a minor league team in Round Rock, Texas. He named it the Express.

Cool cards
You would need a big binder to keep all of the hundreds of Nolan Ryan cards that were made.

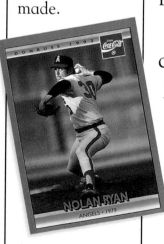

A new league was no problem for the Ryan Express. He led the N.L. in strikeouts, including in 1988, when he was 41, the oldest man to lead that league in strikeouts. (Two years later, he topped himself...leading the A.L. at the age of 43!)

The next stop for the Ryan Express was back home. The Texas Rangers played their home games in Arlington, not far from little Alvin, Texas, Ryan's hometown.

With the Rangers, the Ryan legend grew. As he got older, he got better, punching out batters as regularly as he had when he was in his twenties.

Finally, in 1993, Anaheim catcher Greg Myers became the 5,714th strikeout victim in Ryan's career. Ryan retired as the all-time Strikeout King.

Here are a few more amazing Ryan strikeout numbers:

He had 10 or more strikeouts in a game an awesome 215 times; in 26 of those games, he topped 15 strikeouts!

In 1999, Ryan was elected to the Baseball Hall of Fame in Cooperstown, New York.

The rip-roaring Ryan Express had come to its final stop.

LYNN NOLAN RYAN JR.
NEW YORK, N.L., 1966, 1968–1971
CALIFORNIA, A.L., 1972–1979
HOUSTON, N.L., 1980–1988
TEXAS, A.L., 1989–1993

A FIERCE COMPETITOR AND ONE OF BASEBALL'S MOST INTIMIDATING FIGURES ON THE PITCHING MOUND FOR FOUR DECADES. HIS OVERPOWERING FASTBALL AND UNPARALLELED LONGEVITY PRODUCED 324 VICTORIES AND A HOST OF MAJOR LEAGUE RECORDS. LIFETIME BENCHMARKS INCLUDE 5,714 STRIKEOUTS, SEVEN NO-HITTERS AND 12 ONE-HITTERS IN 27 SEASONS PITCHED. LED LEAGUE IN STRIKEOUTS 11 TIMES AND FANNED 300 BATTERS IN A SEASON ON SIX OCCASIONS, INCLUDING A RECORD 383 IN 1973. STRIKEOUT VICTIMS TOTALED 1,176 DIFFERENT PLAYERS. A TEXAS LEGEND WHOSE WIDESPREAD POPULARITY EXTENDED FAR BEYOND HIS NATIVE STATE.

New home
This plaque in the Baseball Hall of Fame lists Ryan's many amazing records and feats.

Bronzed
Back home in Alvin, the place where he grew up, the town put up a statue of the Strikeout King.

Ryan holds the Major League record for seasons played, with 27.

Who's Next?

Nolan Ryan is in the Hall of Fame, and Roger Clemens, Randy Johnson, and Pedro Martinez will probably join him.

But what other pitchers today are strikeout kings?

Philadelphia's Curt Schilling is one. In 1997, he set a National League record for strikeouts by a righthanded pitcher with 319. He had 300 more in 1998.

Houston relief pitcher Billy Wagner doesn't get a lot of strikeouts in a game. That's because he usually only pitches an inning or so. But that inning is dynamite. Though he's not as tall as many pitchers, Wagner's left arm has big speed.

Kevin Brown This Dodgers pitcher mixed a strong fastball and a super curveball to strike out more than 200 batters in a season seven times.

What an arm! Billy Wagner averages more than 14 strikeouts for every nine innings he pitches. Along with a blazing fastball, he has a great curveball.

Will anyone ever top Ryan, the Rocket, the Big Unit, or Pedro?

Maybe a future Strikeout King is pitching in your youth league this weekend. Maybe that Strikeout King is you!

W.... .id!
In 1998, rookie Kerry Wood of the Chicago Cubs matched Roger Clemens' all-time record with 20 strikeouts in one game.

Schilling
Philadelphia's Curt Schilling has dominated National League hitters for several seasons, with a great fastball and super control.

Glossary

Batter's box
The area to the left or right of home plate where the batter must stand while batting.

Batting helmet
Hard plastic hat that must be worn by batters and baserunners to protect their heads from batted or thrown balls.

Bullpen
An area of the baseball field where relief pitchers warm up and wait their turn to come in.

Called strike
A pitch that goes through the strike zone without the batter swinging and is called a strike by the umpire.

Closer
The last relief pitcher a team uses in a game when they're ahead. Usually he pitches only the ninth inning.

Control
A pitcher has good control when he throws a lot of strikes. His control is off when he walks too many batters.

Curveball
A pitch thrown with an outward snap of the wrist, causing the ball to change direction in flight.

Cy Young Award
Given to the top pitcher in each of the American and National Leagues. Named for all-time wins leader.

Designated hitter
In the American League, pitchers do not bat. Instead this player, also called the D.H., bats in his place. The D.H. does not play in the field.

Hall of Fame
Located in Cooperstown, New York, this building and library complex houses baseball's memories and honors the game's greatest players.

Hurlers
Slang term for pitchers. Hurl means to throw.

Mound
Raised, circular pile of dirt at center of infield from which pitcher pitches.

Perfect game
A rare and awesome pitching feat: Holding a team to zero baserunners for an entire game. Has happened less than 20 times in Major League history.

Radar gun (RAY-dar)
Electronic device used by scouts, coaches, and teams to measure the speed of a pitch. The fastest pitchers can top 100 miles per hour, according to the radar gun.

Relief pitcher
A player who takes over after a starting pitcher leaves the game.

Screwball
A curving pitch thrown by twisting the wrist and hand inward as the ball is released. Very difficult to throw, and hard to hit when thrown well.

Starting pitcher
The player who is the first pitcher for a team in a game.

Whiff
Slang term for when a batter swings and misses; also means a strikeout.

World Series
Postseason championship series of Major League Baseball; played in October as the best of seven games.

Index

All-Star Game 20, 28, 37

Arizona Diamondbacks 28, 30-31

Atlanta Braves 23

Baseball Hall of Fame 45, 46

"Big Unit, The" 24, 29 30-31, 40, 47

Boston Red Sox 16, 18-19, 32, 34

Brown, Kevin 46

Buhner, Jay 32

California Angels 43

Carlton, Steve 15, 40

Clemens, Roger 16, 18-23, 40, 46

Cleveland Indians 11

Cy Young Award 7, 11, 15, 16, 18-19, 21, 28-29, 30, 37

Detroit Tigers 13, 21

Dominican Republic 32, 34

ERA 10, 11, 13, 21, 29, 36-37, 42

Feller, Bob 10-11

Fenway Park 19, 38-39

Gibson, Bob 12-13

Green Monster 19

Griffey, Ken Jr. 32

Houston Astros 30, 42-43

Johnson, Randy 24, 25-31, 40, 46

Johnson, Walter 9, 40

Keefe, Tim 6

Koufax, Sandy 11, 12, 13, 40

Leyritz, Jim 29

Los Angeles Dodgers 34-35

Marichal, Juan 36

Martinez, Pedro 4, 32, 34-39, 40, 46-47

Martinez, Ramon 35, 38

Mathewson, Christy 8-9, 40

McDowell, Sam 12

McGwire, Mark 26, 37

Montreal Expos 27, 35

Newhouser, Hal 21

New York Giants 4

New York Mets 14-15, 40, 41-42

New York Yankees 22-23

Niekro, Phil and Joe 35

no-hitter 10-11, 26-27, 42

Philadelphia Phillies 15

playoffs 18, 22, 29 30, 38

radar gun 9, 14

Ramirez, Manny 32

Red Rock Express 44

release point 24

"Rocket, The" 16, 40, 47

Rusie, Amos 6

Ruth, Babe 4

Ryan, Nolan 11, 40, 42-44,

St. Louis Cardinals 12-13

Schilling, Curt 47

Seattle Mariners 27

Seaver, Tom 14-15

Sosa, Sammy 37

Texas Rangers 40, 44

Toronto Blue Jays 21

Triple Crown 20-21, 36

Trojans 26

umpire 5, 10

University of Southern California 26

University of Texas 16

Vaughn, Mo 29

Waddell, Rube 8

Wagner, Billy 46

Walker, Larry 28

Wood, Kerry 47

World Series 11, 13 14-15, 16, 21, 22-23

World Series ring 23

Yankee Stadium 22

Yastrzemski, Carl 20

Young, Cy 7, 40